T0015399

Last Night
When We Were Young

Last Night
When We Were Young

*Standards and Sambas
from Broadway
to Brazil*

E. J. Rosenblum

PELICAN PUBLISHING
NEW ORLEANS

ISBN 9781455627653

Printed in the United States of America

Published by Pelican Publishing
New Orleans, LA
www.pelicanpub.com

In fact, if you can't manage to put tinges of Spanish in your tune, you will never be able to get the right seasoning, for jazz.

—Jelly Roll Morton

The only countries that really swing in their music are the US, Cuba, and Brazil.

—Antonio Carlos Jobim

Bossa Nova is like those stately homes they used to build out of first-rate materials, things that last forever.

—Marcos Valle

Of thee I sing.

—George and Ira Gershwin

Civilization is seduction.

—Bernard Henri-Levy

I'm not conceited; I'm convinced.

—Little Richard

The song is ended, but the melody lingers on.

—Irving Berlin

Van Heusen's songs sound as though they were written this morning.

—Wilfrid Sheed, *The House That George Built*

The idea that you would do something just for the momentary blissful escape of it, for intensity, for strong feeling, is out of fashion.

—Katie Roiphe, *New York Times*

Well, you needn't.

—Thelonious Monk

Contents

Introduction

Tonal memories: David Clayton Thomas belting "Great God in heaven. . . ." with Blood, Sweat, and Tears on a Sony Walkman, coming home on the West End Boulevard bus. Chicago's "Hollywood" on the St. Charles streetcar.

John Lennon said, "I am not interested in wallpaper, which most music is." What interested me was a memorable melody, a lilt, a great arrangement. A song that hadn't been spun to death on the radio. What stood out without being far out; what made an impression, softly. Beautiful but not banal. To learn what patience and persistence yields. The joy of hearing a sublime Cole Porter for the first time and feeling a "wow" to myself. I was fortunate to be born in New Orleans, northern most point of the tropics, in 1956. Hearing Allen Toussaint at Rosy's on Tchoupitoulas Street, with two tables of pretty ladies by the stage—his guests. Seeing Sonny Rollins at the Fairgrounds on a sunny, breezy afternoon, calypsoing in a tent, with two Rollins moving vans backdropping. One doesn't forget the perfect timing of a Peggy Lee (Basin St. Blues/Quincy Jones/Capitol) or the phrasing of Carmen McRae on "Moonlight in Vermont" from live at Ronnie Scott's. Tony Bennett said that "A Taste of Honey" is a terrific folk song. His certainly is.

I'd like to put forward Candeias and Pra Dizer Adeus from Edu and Bethiana on Elenco/Universal from 1966 with Edu, Maria Bethiana, Edson Machado, and Dorio Ferreira. As well as: So Saudade: "Inutil Paizagem" (Jobim-A.

Oliveira) Danilo Caymmi, Edison Machado, Dori Caymmi, Nana Caymmi, Tom Jobim, Dorival Caymmi, 1964. From Caymmi Vista Tom (Universal/ Elenco/Jasrac). And "Pra Dizer Ade" from Edu and Bethina, 1966, Elenco. Finally, Bud Powell's "Lullaby in Rhythm" (Verve) swings; Peggy Lee's version swivels (Capitol).

Columbia—If one hears the sound of a young man in a wet suit, harpoon in hand, pursuing an eight-hundred-pound jewfish off the coast of Ipanema— that would be the pliant guitar and arrangement of Roberto Menescal. This is not Franz' list; but it is sad, sexy, and syncopated. A passion for exploring the American Songbook and the *New York Times* demanded that I share these gems with you. *Voce!*

A Slice of the Great American Songbook
1920-2020

1) Whose Baby Are You? (Jerome Kern, music) George Gershwin, piano, May 1920. From The Unforgettable Music of Jerome Kern on Avid Records/MP3.

2) My Sweet (Hoagy-Carmichael-Stuart Gorrell) Louis Armstrong and Orchestra, 1930, Okeh label. From Louis Armstrong/Portrait of the Artist as a Young Man on Columbia/Legacy. Armstrong recorded this minor Carmichael composition nineteen months prior to Stardust and Lazy River. He sings and plays as someone out of the market last October of '29.

3) Raisin the Rent (Harold Arlen-Ted Koehler) Duke Ellington, Ivie Anderson, Harry Carney, Cootie Williams, Sam Nanton, 1933, Columbia. From Duke Ellington Presents Ivie Anderson.

4) Got a Bran' New Suit (Desmond Carter, Vivien Ellis) Fats Waller & Co., 1935. From The Centennial Collection, Bluebird.

5) Hittin' the Bottle (Harold Arlen-Ted Koehler) Jimmy Lunceford, Sy Oliver, Eddie Durham, Willie Smith, et al., 1935. From Jimmie Lunceford and His Orchestra: For Dancers Only, on Decca. Lunceford's band was rivaled only by Duke Ellington's Orchestra in 1935. In February, Lunceford grossed $42,000 in one week at the Metropolitan Theater in Boston.

6) Remember (Irving Berlin) Red Norvo. Arr: Eddie Sauter,1937. From Red Norvo: Jivin' the Jeep on Hep label.

7) I'll Never Be the Same (Matty Melneck, Frank Signorelli, Gus Kahn) Billie Holiday, Teddy Wilson, Buck Clayton, Lester Young, Freddie Green, Walter Page, Jo Jones, 1937. From The Complete Billie Holiday Mastertakes Collection 1933/42 by Allesandro Protti Vol. 3/1937 on King Jazz. Has the most vibrant sound with the most "pres"ence among the imports. Columbia's 2002 remastering for the compilation Billie Holiday and Lester Young: A Musical Romance on Columbia/Legacy is fine.

8) Love Walked In (George and Ira Gershwin) Louis Armstrong, 1938. From Pocketful of Dreams: Louis Armstrong and His Orchestra, Decca.

9) Me and You (Edward Kennedy Ellington). Ellington, Ivie Anderson, Cootie Williams, Ray Nance, Rex Stewart, Lawrence Brown, Juan Tizol, Barney Bigard, Johnny Hodges, Harry Carney, 1940. From An Introduction to Ivie Anderson—Best of Jazz—The Swing Era. Superior sound to Bluebird recording.

10) Robbins' Nest (Sir Charles Thompson-Illinois Jacquet) Ella Fitzgerald, Hank Jones, Ray, Brown, and Buddy Rich. Carnegie Hall, 1949. From Ultimate Ella Fitzgerald on Verve.

11) Can't Get Out of This Mood (Jimmy McHugh-Frank Loesser) Sarah Vaughan, Miles Davis, Tony Scott, Budd Johnson, Jimmy Jones, Freddie Green, Billy Taylor Sr., and J. C. Heard, 1950. From Sarah Vaughan/The Complete Columbia Singles on Acrobat label. Acrobat's 2019 compilation remastering reveals what my older Columbia copy couldn't. Samara Joy and her trio render a fine version of this song in 2023, from Linger Awhile (Verve).

12) Why Do I Love You? (Jerome Kern) Charlie Parker, Walter Bishop Jr., Jose Mangual, Roy Haynes, 1951. From the album South of the Border on Verve. Also, Charlie Parker Plays Standards on Verve. "It was a sound that was, as they say, devoid of pity."—Stanley Crouch

13) On a Slow Boat to China (Frank Loesser) Sonny Rollins, Kenny Drew, Percy Heath, Art Blakey, 1951, Prestige label. The last thing I noticed, years later, was the humor in the pace vs. the song title.

14) Blue Moon (Richard Rodgers-Larry Hart) Billie Holiday, Oscar Peterson, Flip Philips, Ray Brown, 1952. From the album Solitude on Verve.

15) You Turned the Tables on Me (Louis Alter-Sidney D. Mitchell) Billie Holiday, Oscar Peterson, Flip Philips, Ray Brown, 1952. From the album Solitude on Verve.

16) Memphis in June (Hoagy Carmichael-Paul Francis Webster) Johnny Mercer, 1952, Capitol. From Stardust-Capitol Sings Hoagy Carmichael. Also on American Songbook Series/Hoagy Carmichael on Smithsonian Collection Recordings. Johnny Mercer paid off all his father's debts; he was Harold Arlen's coolest lyricist. Mercer would come to Arlen's apartment in Manhattan, to have Arlen open the door with, "Hello, cloud boy."

17) Miles Ahead (Miles Davis) Davis, John Lewis, Max Roach, Percy Heath, 1953. From Miles Davis: Blue Haze on Prestige Records. Not to be confused with later Columbia versions.

18) Hymn of the Orient (Gigi Gryce) Clifford Brown, Gigi Gryce, Charles Rouse, John Lewis, Percy Heath, Art Blakey, 1953. From Clifford Brown memorial Album. Blue Note.

19) This Can't Be Love (Rodgers-Hart) Lester Young Quintet, 1953. From The Complete Lester Young Studio Sessions on Verve.

20) Long Ago and Far Away (Jerome Kern) Chet Baker, Russ Freeman, Carson Smith, and Bob Neal. From the album Chet Baker, Boston, 1954. Performed at George Wein's Storyville Club, Copley Square Hotel. Kern hated having his songs jazzed up; the three on this page are so sophisticated, however.

21) The Way You Look Tonight (Jerome Kern) Thelonious Monk, Sonny Rollins, Percy Heath, Art Taylor. Prestige RVG remasters, 1954. Rollins is brimming.

22) There's a Small Hotel (Rodgers-Hart) Art Tatum, 1954. From Art Tatum Solo Masterpieces/Pablo.

23) I've Got a Feeling I'm Falling (Fats Waller-Billy Rose) Louis Armstrong, Billy Kyle, Trummy Young, Barney Bigard, Barrett Deems, Arvell Shaw, 1955, Columbia. Also on a Japanese import.

24) Little Melonae (Jackie McLean) Miles Davis, John Coltrane, Red Garland, Paul Chambers, Philly Joe Jones, 1955. From 'Round About Midnight on Columbia/Legacy.

25) Of Thee I Sing (George and Ira Gershwin) Stan Getz, Lou Levy, Shelly Manne, Leroy Vinnegar. From Stan Getz and the Cool Sounds, 1955, Verve.

26) I See Your Face Before Me (Arthur Schwartz-Howard Dietz) Miles Davis, Red Garland, Oscar Pettiford, Philly Joe Jones, 1955. From The Musings of Miles on Prestige.

27) Will You Still Be Mine? (Tom Adair-Matt Dennis) Miles Davis, Red Garland, Oscar Pettiford, Philly Joe Jones, 1955. From The Musings of Miles on Prestige. Also on The Definitive Miles Davis on Prestige.

28) Sad Walk (Bob Zieff) Chet Baker, Dick Twardzik, James Bond, Peter Littman. 1955. From the Complete Barclay Recordings of Chet Baker Volume 1. Emarcy label.

29) Cuban Blues (Chico O'Farrill) Chico O'Farrill, 1956. From Cuban Blues on Verve.

30) Night and Day (Cole Porter) Art Tatum, Ben Webster, Red Callender, Bill Douglas, 1956. From Art Tatum: The Complete Pablo Group Masterpieces. Tatum's style is well suited for Porter's wit, romanticism, and *joie de vivre* recorded in his last year. Tatum goes for baroque, while Webster is relaxed.

31) My Ideal (Richard Whiting) Art Tatum, Ben Webster, et al., 1956. As above. Whiting's (Too Marvelous for Words) favorite song. "Will I ever find the girl in my mind, the one who is my ideal?" Hear Tony Bennett and Ralph Sharon's duet of this.

32) Almost Like Being in Love (Lerner-Loewe) Lester Young Quartet in Washington, DC, 1956. On Pablo. Perhaps Pablo will re-release in a label compilation of gems. There are two versions of this standard in this five volume set, and this is the peach of the set.

33) When Lights Are Low (Benny Carter) Miles Davis, Red Garland, John Coltrane, Paul Chambers, Philly Joe Jones, 1956 (not to be confused with

the shorter 1953 version on Blue Haze). From The Definitive Miles Davis on Prestige.

34) It's Bad for Me (Cole Porter) Rosemary Clooney, Benny Goodman, 1956. RCA/Columbia.

35) Someday You'll Want Me (Dave Bartholomew-Pearl King) Smiley Lewis, 1956. From The Big Beat of Dave Bartholomew on EMI. Also on The New Orleans R & B of Smiley Lewis on Jasmine Records.

36) Count Your Blessings (Irving Berlin) Sonny Rollins, Max Roach, Richie Powell, George Morrow, 1956, Prestige. From Sonny Rollins Plus Four. A masterpiece, stripped of sentimentality.

37) Undecided (Charlie Shavers, Sid Robins) Ray Charles, Fathead Newman, et al, 1956. Arr: Quincy Jones and Ernie Wilkins, Atlantic Records.

38) I Guess I'll Have to Change My Plan (Schwartz-Dietz) Sinatra/Riddle, 1956, Capitol. From A Swingin' Affair, 1984 remastering.

39) Exactly Like You (Jimmy McHugh-Dorothy Fields) Carmen McRae, 1957. From After Glow on Decca. Go for the Japanese import; beautiful clarity. "No one ever took greater care with a lyric."—Mel Torme

40) Perdido (Juan Tizol, H. J. Lengsfelder) Carmen McRae, Ike Issacs, Specs Wright, 1957. From After Glow on Decca. Go for the Japanese import.

41) Jitterbug Waltz (Fats Waller, Maxine Manners, Charles Green) Dinah Washington, Clark Terry, Charlie Shavers, Joe Newman, Ernie Royal, Julian Priester, Melba Liston, Jerome Richardson, Sahib Shihab, Frank Wess, Benny Golson, Freddie Green. Arr: Ernie Wilkins, 1957, Emarcy. Also on Smithsonian Recordings of Fats Waller. An impressive pile-up.

42) Just One of Those Things (Cole Porter) Louis Armstrong, Oscar Peterson, Ray Brown, Louis Bellson, 1957, Verve Master edition. From Louis Armstrong Meets Oscar Peterson

43) I've Got the World on a String (Harold Arlen-Ted Koehler) Henry "Red" Allen, Buster Bailey, Coleman Hawkins, Marty Napoleon, Cozy Cole. RCA/

Bluebird, 1957. Also on a Coleman Hawkins Bluebird collection.

44) 365 Igrejas (Dorival Caymmi) Dorival Caymmi. From Raizes do Samba on EMI, 1957.

45) Violets for Your Furs (Matt Dennis-Tom Adair) John Coltrane, Johnnie Splawn, Sahib Shihab, Red Garland, Paul Chambers, Albert Heath, 1957. From Coltrane/Prestige 7105. I believe Sinatra proposed to one of his wives in front of Rockefeller Square with this song.

46) Stompin' at The Savoy (Benny Goodman, Edgar Sampson, Check Webb, Andy Razaf) Ella Fitzgerald, Louis Armstrong, Oscar Peterson, Ray Brown, Herb Ellis, Louis Bellson. From Ella and Louis Again, 1957, Verve.

47) Star Eyes (Raye-DePaul) Art Pepper, Red Garland, Paul Chambers, Philly Joe Jones, 1957. From Art Pepper Meets the Rhythm Section. OJC Remasters/Contemporary label.

48) For All We Know (Sam H. Lewis-J. Fred Coots) Dave Brubeck, Paul Desmond, Eugene Wright, Joe Morello, 1957. From Monterey Jazz Festival: 40 Legendary Years. Warner Bros. A special, more concise version than his live Columbia recording.

49) Dancing in the Dark (Schwartz-Dietz) Duke Ellington, Cat Anderson, Ray Nance, Jimmy Hamilton, Russell Procope, Johnny Hodges, Paul Gonsalves, Harry Carney, Jimmy Woode, Sam Woodyard, 1957. From The Complete Ellington Indigos/Phoenix Records. & Ellington Indigos/Columbia.

50) How's Chances? (Irving Berlin) Ella Fitzgerald, Ted Nash, Paul Smith, Alvin Stoller, 1958, Hollywood. Arr: Paul Weston. From Cheek to Cheek: The Irving Berlin Songbook on Verve. Also on Ella Fitzgerald/The Irving Berlin Songbook: Volume 2. "My mother sang what Ella Fitzgerald sang."—Toni Morrison

51) Like Someone in Love (Jimmy Van Heusen-Johnny Burke) Sarah Vaughn, Thad Jones, Henry Coker, Frank Wess, Ronnell Bright, Richard Davis, Roy Haynes, 1958, Mercury. From James Van Heusen/Smithsonian Collection of Recordings. Perfectly shoe-horned from a live set with great sound.

52) I Hadn't Anyone Till You (Ray Noble) Mose Allison, Addison Farmer, 1958.

From Mose Allison Sings, Prestige. "Musically American by adoption."—Alec Wilder

53) I've Told Ev'ry Little Star (Jerome Kern) Sonny Rollins, Barney Kessell, Hampton Hawes, Shelly Manne, Red Mitchell, 1958, Contemporary/Riverside/Prestige. Oscar Hammerstein II sang this song to Jerome Kern as Kern lay dying.

54) You Make Me Feel So Young (Myrow-Gordon) (take five) Chet Baker, Kenny Drew, Sam Jones, Philly Joe Jones. From Chet Baker Sings—It Could Happen to You—Original Jazz Classics Remasters, 1958, Riverside.

55) Fathead (David Newman) from Fathead: Ray Charles presents David Newman, 1958, on Atlantic. Incl. Hank Crawford, Marcus Belgrave, and Ray Charles.

56) Then I'll Be Tired of You (Schwartz-Yip Harburg) John Coltrane, Red Garland, Art Taylor, Paul Chambers, Freddie Hubbard, 1958. From the album Stardust on Prestige. Sublime.

57) What Is There to Say? (Vernon Duke-Yip Harburg) Bill Evans, Sam Jones, Philly Joe Jones, December 15, 1958. From Everybody Digs Bill Evans/Keepnews Collection, Riverside.
Vladimir Dukelsky, a White Russian, was trained as a musical prodigy from the age of four. Composer of the music to Autumn in New York, and I Can't Get Started, Duke—a difficult adult—was introduced to Yip Harburg by Ira Gershwin. George had him change his name, loaned him money on more than one occasion, and bought him a piano, according to Wilfrid Sheed in *The House That George Built.*

58) Peri's Scope (Bill Evans) Evans, Scott LaFaro, and Paul Motian, December 28, 1959, NYC. From Portrait in Jazz/Keepnews Collection. Basquiat favored be bop.

59) U.M.M.G. (Upper Manhattan Medical Group) (Billy Strayhorn) Dizzy Gillespie, Duke Ellington, Clark Terry, Cat Anderson, Shorty Baker, Johnny Hodges, Paul Gonsalves, Harry Carney, Jimmy Hamilton, Russell Procope, Britt Woodman, Quentin Jackson, Jimmy Jones, Jimmy Woode, Sam Woodyard. 1959 from Ellington Jazz Party on Columbia

60) Let's Fall in Love (Harold Arlen-Ted Koehler) Ella Fitzgerald. Arr: Frank DeVol, 1959. From Ella Fitzgerald Sings Sweet Songs for Swingers. Verve, 2016 remastering. Fitzgerald recorded this standard a year or two later for The Harold Arlen Songbook. This arrangement is less kinetic, more relaxed than the subsequent arrangement by Billy May. Sung straight.

61) The Half of It, Dearie Blues (George and Ira Gershwin) Ella Fitzgerald, Buddy Collette, Harry Klee et al., 1959. Arr: Nelson Riddle. From The George and Ira Gershwin Songbook on Verve. No strings attached.

62) I Was Doing Alright (George and Ira Gershwin) Annie Ross, Zoot Sims, Russ Freeman, Jim Hall, Mel Lewis, 1959. From the album A Gasser! On Pacific Jazz. Also on Japanese import. Oscar and Louis produced the great red beans and rice version; this is the looser, more swingin' version—the gasser!

63) So In Love (Cole Porter) Peggy Lee, 1959. From I Like Men! Capitol Records.

64) Saudade Fez Um Samba (Carlos Lyra-Ronaldo Boscoli) Joao Gilberto, Tom Jobim, Milton Banana, 1959. From Chega de Saudade, el/Cherry Red Records.

65) E Luxo So (It Is Luxury) (Ary Barroso-Luis Peixoto) Joao Gilberto, Milton Banana, 1959. From Chega de Saudade. el/Cherry Red Records. Predates Byrd/Getz by three years.

66) Aos Pes Da Cruz (Marino Pinto-Zeda Zilda) Joao Gilberto, Milton Banana, 1959. From Chega de Saudade, el/Cherry Red Records.

67) Dois De Fevereiro (Dorival Caymmi) from Caymmi e seu violao, 1959, Odeon. Also on Raises do Samba compilation on EMI.

68) Learnin' the Blues (Dolores Silver) Oscar Peterson, Ray Brown, and Ed Thigpen. Paris, May 1959. From A Jazz Portrait of Frank Sinatra on Verve.

69) I Used to Be Color Blind (Irving Berlin) Oscar Peterson Trio, 1959. From The Song Books, Verve.

70) Take the A Train (Billy Strayhorn) Oscar Peterson Trio, 1959. From The Song Books, Verve.

71) Without a Song (Vincent Youmans) Oscar Peterson Trio, 1959. From The Song Books, Verve.

72) Long Ago and Far Away (Jerome Kern) Oscar Peterson Trio, 1959. From The Song Books, Verve.

73) You'll Never Know (Harry Warren) Oscar Peterson Trio, 1959. From The Song Books, Verve.

74) It Ain't Necessarily So (George and Ira Gershwin) Oscar Peterson Trio. From Oscar Peterson Plays Porgy and Bess/Verve, 1959. Not to be confused with the earlier recording from The Song Books. This version, recorded in October, is a minute longer, looser, and bluesier.

75) Strange Meadowlark (Dave and Iola Brubeck) Dave Brubeck, Carmen McRae, Eugene Wright, Joe Morello, 1960. From Dave Brubeck Quartet/ guest star/Carmen McRae/Tonight Only! On American Jazz Classics.

76) By Myself (Schwartz-Dietz) Rosemary Clooney/Nelson Riddle, 1960, RCA/Capitol.

77) You Stepped Out of a Dream (Nacio Herb Brown-Gus Kahn) Sarah Vaughan, Sweets Edison, Jimmy Jones, 1960. From the album The Divine One on Roulette/Blue Note/EMI. *Avoid* low-fidelity Hallmark budget label.

78) Remember (Irving Berlin) Hank Mobley, Art Blakey, Wynton Kelly, and Paul Chambers, 1960. From Soul Station on Blue Note.

79) Coffee Time (Harry Warren-Arthur Freed) Carmen Mc Rae and Andre Previn Trio, 1960. From The Subterraneans soundtrack. Also on The Hollywood Swing and Jazz compilation.

80) Jeannine (Duke Pearson) Cannonball Adderly, Nat Adderly, Barry Harris, Sam Jones, Louis Hayes, 1960. From Them Dirty Blues on Capitol Jazz.

81) Black Beauty (Duke Ellington). From The Essential Ellington 1960 Columbia Legacy.

82) Imagination (Jimmy Van Heusen-Johnny Burke) Dean Martin/Nelson

Riddle, 1960. From Spotlight on Dean Martin/Great Gentlemen of Song on Capitol.

83) Oo-Bla-Dee (Mary Lou Williams) Junior Mance Trio, 1960. From The Soulful Piano of Junior Mance. Jazzland/Riverside Import Japan. Also on Fresh Sound Records. Acrobat's compilation will be a bit compressed.

84) Doralice (Dorival Caymmi-Antonio Almeida) Joao Gilberto, Tom Jobim, and Milton Banana (sans Stan Getz), 1960. From O amor, o sorriso e a flor on el/Cherry Red Records. Precedes Getz/Gilberto by a few years.

> Bossa Nova overwhelmed us. What Joao Gilberto proposed was a deeply penetrating and highly personal interpretation of the spirit of samba. He did this through a mechanically simple but musically challenging guitar beat that suggested an infinite variety of subtle ways to make the vocal phrasing swing over a harmony of chords progressing in a fluent equilibrium. And in so doing, he ignited the combustible elements of a revolution that was not only to make possible the whole evolution of Antonio Carlos Jobim, Carlos Lyra, Newton Mendonca, Joao Donato, Ronaldo Boscoli and Sergio Ricardo—his generational peers—but also to open the way for emerging younger musicians such as Roberto Menescal, Sergio Mendes, Nara Leao, Baden Powell, and Leny Andrade.
>
> In Caymmi the sung word received the loftiest treatment imaginable: always spontaneous, it nevertheless reveals the rigorous scrutiny it has undergone. Caymmi's songs seem to exist of their own accord, but the perfection of their simplicity, attained through precision in the choice of words and notes, is the mark of an exacting author. They are how a song ought to be, how good songs have always been and always will be. A Tuva song, a lied by Schubert, a Gershwin ballad, the "Dying Eagle" by Ives, must be compared with "Sargaco Mar," "La Vem A Baiana" and "Voce Ja Foi A Bahia": they are all incursions into the essential reality of song. This is how Joao's great modernization came to build on Caymmi's effortless modernization. At once impressionistic and primitive, the greatest inventor of urban-modern samba, Caymmi weights as heavily on the Joao Gilbertian elaboration on bossa nova as Orlando Silva, Ciro Monteiro, American music from the thirties, and cool jazz—while possessing more gravity. Everything in Joao pays homage to him. From his sense of structure to his diction.
>
> The way that Joao Gilberto heard Caymmi and cultivated the standard he set for the world as song—this is the selective filter of bossa nova; it is the source of the torque in Tom Jobim's music and the poetry in that of Vinicius.
>
> —*Tropical Truth; a Story of Music and Revolution in Brazil* by Caetano Veloso (Knopf, 2002)

85) Discussao (Jobim-Newton Mendonca) Joao Gilberto, Tom Jobim, Milton

Banana, 1960. From O amor, or sorriso e a flor on el/Cherry Red Records.

86) Brigas, Nunca Mais (Jobim-De Moraes) Paulino Nogueira. From Homenagem a Antonio Carlos Jobim/Instrumental 3, 1960, on RGE. Quietly ecstatic to see this still available on Amazon. Archetypal.

87) Ooh Poo Pah Doo (part two) (Jesse Hill) Hill, Allen Toussaint, David Lastie, John Boudreaux, 1960, Minit/EMI. From Finger Poppin' and Stompin' Feet on Crescent City Soul. Arr. and produced by Allen Toussaint.

88) Teo (Miles Davis) John Coltrane, Wynton Kelly, Paul Chambers, Jimmy Cobb, 1961. From Miles Davis/Someday My Prince Will Come, Columbia/Legacy. Produced by Teo Macero. Crisp like a clean linen shirt.

89) Ill Wind (Harold Arlen-Ted Koehler) Oscar Peterson, Ray Brown, and Ed Thigpen. From Oscar Peterson Trio Live at the London House, 1961, Verve. One hears Tatum's influence at the outset.

90) Alone Together (Schwartz-Dietz) Joe Williams, Harry "Sweets" Edison on Roulette and Jazz Masters/Warner/Japan, 1961. From Joe Williams and Sweets Edison: Together.

91) There's a Small Hotel (Rodgers-Hart) Joe Williams, Harry "Sweets" Edison on Roulette and Jazz Masters/Warner/Japan, 1961. From Joe Williams and Sweets Edison: Together.

92) I Should Care (Cahn-Stordahl-West) Hank Mobley, Wynton Kelly, Paul Chambers, Philly Joe Jones, 1961. From Hank Mobley: Another Workout, Blue Note. "I should go around weeping"—Sammy Cahn. There are many versions of this song and many Hank Mobley tracks.

93) Yesterdays (Jerome Kern-Otto Harbach) Carmen McRae, Cannonball Adderly, Norman Simmons, Lockjaw Davis, 1961, on Columbia/Legacy. From Loverman and Other Billie Holiday Classics. *Avoid* low-fidelity budget label. A great standard with a performance/recording for the ages.

94) Alice in Wonderland (take two) (Sammy Fain) Bill Evans, Scott LaFaro, and Paul Motian. From Sunday at the Village Vanguard. Riverside/Keepnews Collection, June 1961

95) Off Minor (Thelonious Monk) Bud Powell, Pierre Michelot, Kenny Clarke, Paris 1961. From A Portrait of Thelonious Monk, Columbia

96) Evening in Paris (Victor Feldman) Stan Getz, Victor Feldman, Louis Hayes, Sam Jones, 1961. From The Very Best of Stan Getz on Verve. Also on Stan Getz: Best of the Verve Years
"Let's face it, we'd all sound like Stan Getz . . . if we could"—John Coltrane

97) It Was Written in the Stars (Harold Arlen-Leo Robin) Ella Fitzgerald, Don Fagerquist, 1961. From Ella Fitzgerald: The Harold Arlen Songbook, Vol. 2, Verve. The Schubertian side of Arlen.

98) You Swing Baby (The Duke) (Dave Brubeck) Louis Armstrong, Dave Brubeck, Carmen McRae, Billy Kyle, Gene Wright, Joe Morello, 1961. Supervised by Teo Macero. To be found on The Complete Louis Armstrong Columbia and RCA Victor Studio Sessions 1946-1966, Columbia/RCA Victor/ Mosaic 2020 compilation. Mosaic paid a premium to Sony to get this song.

99) My Man's Gone Now (George Gershwin-Dubose Heyward) Bill Evans, Scott La Faro, and Paul Motian, 1961. There are two slightly different recordings of the same performance. Scott LaFaro's clean intro framing a definitive standard perfectly and the other that begins with a few seconds of clapping. This intro ruins it for me. It's like a canvas with no frame and a beautiful artwork with a nice border. From The Famous Bill Evans Trio: Sunday at the Village Vanguard. The recordings you want would be the Japanese/Jasrac/20-bit remasterings. The tracks with the clapping would be the Keepnews Collection and The Complete Bill Evans: Sunday at the Village Vanguard three-disc box set. The two best things about the newly-issued Everybody Still Digs Bill Evans are the cover photograph in red and the concisely framed recording of My Man's Gone Now.

100) That Old Black Magic (Arlen/Mercer) Dave Brubeck, Tony Bennett. From The Essential Tony Bennett, 1962. Columbia/Legacy.

101) There Are Many Worlds (Jaki Byard) Jaki Byard, Ron Carter, Pete La Roca, 1962. From Jaki Byard: Hi-Fly, on New Jazz. Wonderful.

102) Quiet Nights of Quiet Stars (Corcovado) (Jobim-B. Kaye-Gee Lees) Tony Bennett, 1962. From I Wanna Be Around. Columbia/Legacy.

103) Get Out of Town (Cole Porter) Gerry Mulligan, Tommy Flanagan, Ben Tucker, Dave Bailey, and Alex Dorsey, 1962. From Jeru, on Columbia/Legacy. Regards to Peggy Lee and Caetano Veloso. I first heard this a few years ago and knew my ears had struck gold at first listen.

104) Everything I Love (Cole Porter) Bill Evans, Chuck Israels, Paul Motian, 1962. From How My Heart Sings. OJC remasters.

105) Whisper Not (Benny Golson) Mel Torme, 1962. From "Comin' Home baby!" On Atlantic.

106) Cry Like the Wind (Jule Styne) Coleman Hawkins, Tommy Flanagan, Major Holley, Eddie Locke, 1962. From Make Someone Happy. Moodsville.

107) You Are My Sunshine (Jimmy Davis- Charles Mitchell) Ray Charles, Margie Hendrix, Hank Crawford, Fathead Newman, and the Raelettes, 1962. ABC/Paramount.

108) Java (Toussaint/Tyler/Friday) Al Hirt, 1962. From Honey in the Horn RCA, produced by Chet Atkins and Steve Sholes. Nice fidelity on original disc/lp; fewer tracks than later compilations. Jumbo. Al Hirt sold out Carnegie Hall and played for eight US presidents and Pope Paul II. He gave Wynton Marsalis his first trumpet and lived on Canal Blvd., the last home before Lake Pontchartrain. This hit and Whipped Cream for Herb Albert and the Newlyweds bought our composer/hero his brown and gold Rolls Royce.

109) Contrasts (Jimmy Dorsey) Duke Ellington, Paul Gonsalves, Jimmy Hamilton, Johnny Hodges, Sam Woodyard, 1962. Reprise/Atlantic.

110) Beautiful Love (Victor Young) Jackie McLean, Bobby Timmons, 1962. From Matador: Inta Somethin' on Blue Note, with Kenny Dorham. Best fidelity if you can find the lone Matador disc.

111) Cariba (take two) Wes Montgomery, Johnny Griffin, Wynton Kelly, Paul Chambers, Jimmy Cobb, 1962. From Full House, Riverside/Keepnews Collection.

112) Tune for Duke (Bud Powell) Bud Powell Trio, 1963. From Bud Powell Paris Sessions (Pablo label).

113) Dearly Beloved (Jerome Kern-Johnny Mercer) Nancy Wilson, 1963, Hollywood: Capitol.

114) Any Old Time (Burt Bacharach-Hal David) Dionne Warwick, 1963, Warner/Rhino.
     "I am a Burt Bacharach-Hal David fanatic."—Smokey Robinson

115) Old Devil Moon (E.Y. Harburg, Burton Lane) Sinatra/Riddle, 1963. From The Very Best of Frank Sinatra, Reprise.

116) The Lamp Is Low (Peter DeRose, Bert Shefter, Mitchell Parish) Bill Henderson and the Oscar Peterson Trio, 1963, Verve. Framed by Milestones—very cool.
     "Oscar Peterson is my God."—Andre Watts

117) E Vem O Sol (Marcos Valle-Paulo Sergio Valle) Marcos Valle. Arr: Eumir Deodato, 1963. From Marcos Valle: Samba Demais, EMI.

118) Desafinado (mono version) (Antonio Carlos Jobim-Newton Mendonca) Stan Getz, Joao Gilberto, Tom Jobim, Sebastiao Neto, and Milton Banana. March, 1963. From Getz/Gilberto. Stereo/Mono Verve 2014 remastering. The mono version dials down the bass and percussion, revealing the intoxicating genius.

> With the money he earned from their Getz/Gilberto album, Stan Getz bought a home in Irvington, New York, that had belonged to Francis Gershwin, sister of the late George. It was a Gone with the Wind-style mansion with twenty-three rooms and white two-story columns. Joao Gilberto, as co-star, received $23,000 and a pair of Grammys that he lost. Astrud Gilberto, who sang "Garota de Ipanema" in English and was responsible for the record's international success, earned $120.
> —Ruy Castro, *Bossa Nova: The Story of the Brazilian Music that Seduced the World*

119) Once Again (Outra Vez) (Jobim) Stan Getz, Laurindo Almeida, Edison Machado, George Duvivier, 1963, Verve. 2017 remastering cuts the cheese. "Anywhere in the civilized world, you'll always hear two things: Frank Sinatra and the songs of Antonio Carlos Jobim."—Sammy Cahn

120) Menina Moca (Young Lady) (Luis Antonio) Stan Getz, Laurindo Almeida, Edison Machado, George Duvivier, 1963, Verve. 2017 remastering convinced me.

121, 122) O Barquinho, Errinho Toa (Roberto Menescal-Ronaldo Boscoli) from Lucio Alves/Balancamba, 1963, Elenco/Universal.

123) Voce E Eu (Carlos Lyra-Vinicius De Moraes) Sylvia Telles, Geraldo Vespar, 1963, Elenco. From Bossa Nova Lounge/Corcovado. Dubas Musica.

124) Lobo Bobo (The Big Bad Wolf) (Carlos Lyra-Ronaldo Boscoli) Paul Winter, Carlos Lyra, Sergio Mendes, Sebastiao Neto, Milton Banana, 1964. From Paul Winter with Carlos Lyra: The Sound of Ipanema. Sony Music Japan.

125) Lush Life (Billy Strayhorn) Jaki Byard, Bob Cranshaw, Walter Perkins, 1964. From Jaki Byard: Out Front! Prestige.

126) On a Clear Day (Burton Lane) Oscar Peterson, Sam Jones, Bobby Durham, 1964. MPS/Verve from Girl Talk: Exclusively for My Friends.

127) Wives and Lovers (Bacharach-David) Sinatra, Basie, Sweets, Q, 1964, Concord.

128) Iberia (Dave Brubeck) Brubeck, Eugene Wright, Joe Morello, 1964. From Time Changes, Columbia. Gene Wright died in 2021, the last of the phenomenal four. In his obituary, we read of Wright recalling the quartet playing somewhere in the South and a promoter telling Brubeck he did not want the bassist sharing the stage. When the curtain came up, Brubeck had Wright placed right in front and they came out swinging.

129) So Long, Big Time (Harold Arlen-Dory Previn) Tony Bennett, 1964. From The Many Moods of Tony Bennett, Columbia. There is a nice video of this. "Harold's best is the best"—Irving Berlin

130) Charade (Henry Mancini-Johnny Mercer) Blossom Dearie, 1964. From May I Come In? Capitol.

131) Out of This World (Arlen-Mercer) Tony Bennett, Stan Getz, Herbie Hancock, Ron Carter, Elvin Jones, 1964. From This Is Jazz 33/Tony Bennett, Columbia/Legacy. And it is.

132) The More I See You (Harry Warren- Mack Gordon) Johnny Hartman, Hank Jones, Barry Galbraith, Richard Davis, Osie Johnson, 1964. From The Voice That IS! Impulse/GRP. *Not* the string version, please (on Unforgettable).

133) Voce E Eu (Carlos Lyra- Vinicius DeMoraes) Astrud Gilberto, Stan Getz, Kenny Burrell, Helcio Milito, 1964. From Astud Gilberto Diva Series, Verve.

134) Influencia Do Jazz (Carlos Lyra) Bola Sete, Monty Budwig, and Nick Martinez, 1964. From Voodoo Village, Fantasy Records. Bonito.

135) Mascarada (Ze Keti, Elton Madeiros) Quarteto em Cy, Louiz Carlos Vinhas Trio. Arr: Eumir Deodato, 1964. From Quarteto em Cy. Bomba Records/Jasrac/Tokyo. Also on Bossa Nova Lounge/Ipanema, Dubas Musica. Bomba has high fidelity.

136) Adriana (Luiz Fernando Freire-Roberto Menescal) Wanda Sa, Roberto Menescal, Eumir Deodato, Uge Marotta, 1964. From Wanda Sa/Anos 60 on Discobertas three-disc box set, 2014 remastering.

137) Berimbau (Baden Powell-Vinicius) Dori Caymmi, Danilo Caymmi, Edison Machado, Tom Jobim 1964 from Caymmi visita Tom Universal/ Jasrac (Japanese import has space in between tracks).

138) It Could Happen to You (Johnny Burke-Jimmy Van Heusen) Tony Bennett with the Ralph Sharon Trio, 1964. From When Lights Are Low, RPM Records/Columbia/Legacy. A friend current in this century's technology tells me one can program up to three seconds between tracks when streaming.

139) Because You're Mine (Sammy Cahn-Nicholas Brodszky) Carmen McRae, Barry Galbraith, Arr: Peter Matz, 1964. From Carmen McRae: Second to None. Mainstream Records/Jasrac

140) You'd Be So Nice To Come Home To (Cole Porter) Ella Fitzgerald, Roy Eldridge, Tommy Flanagan 1964 From the album Ella Fitzgerald at Juan Les Pins on Verve

141) Consolacao (Baden Powell-Vinicius DeMoraes) Rosinha de Valenca, Sebastiao Neto, Chico Batera, 1965. From Wanda Sa/Bossa Nova/Anos 60. Three-disc box set on Discobertas 2014 remastering. Powell's greatest disciple.

142, 143, 144) Coisa No. 1, Coisa No. 7, Coisa, No. 6 (Moacir Santos) Santos-Clovis Carmello de Mello) (Santos), 1965. From Coisas/Moacir Santos, Forma.

145) Aruanda (Carlos Lyra-Geraldo Vandre-Norman Gimbel) Astrud Gilberto, 1965, Verve.

146) Samba De Orfeu (Luiz Bonfa) Bonfa, Helcio Milito, and Dom Un Romao. From Braziliana, Universal/Mercury/Jasrac, 1965. Also on The Bossa Nova Encore! Universal/Jasrac.

147) A Morte De Um Deus De Sal (Death of a Sea God) (Roberto Menescal) Luiz Eca and cordas, 1965, on Estrelas Brasilieras series/orig. Philips. Eca, Bebeto, Ohanna, Neco.

148) Photograph (Jobim-DeMoraes) Astrud Gilberto, Tom Jobim, Joao Donato, Bud Shank, Joe Mondragon, 1965. From Astrud Gilberto's Finest Hour, Verve. This compilation has the only track of this "Photograph" with the extra millisecond of Joe Mondragon's bass, a sliver of a frame, before the rush of strings, providing a bit of definition; Tom digs in.

149) Fotografia (Jobim-DeMoraes) Dick Farney, 1965. From The Bossa Nova. Universal/Jasrac Classic.

150) So Nice (Marcos Valle Paulo Sergio Valle-Norman Gimbel) Johnny Mathis, 1965. From The Global Masters, Columbia/Legacy.

151) O Jangadeiro (Dulce Nunes-Joao de Vale) Alaide Costa, 1965. From the compilation "Wave Nos E O Mar," Dubas Musica.

152) Vai De Vez (Roberto Menescal) Rosinha de Valenca, Sergio Mendes, Sebastiao Neto, and Chico Batera, 1965. From In Person at El Matador: Sergio Mendes and Brasil '65. East/West/Japan.

153) April Come She Will (Paul Simon), 1965. From The Paul Simon Songbook, Columbia/Legacy. A more defined recording than the track on Simon and Garfunkel's The Sounds of Silence. Mono.

154) Pensativa (Clare Fischer) from Free For All: Art Blakey and the jazz Messengers, 1965. Blakey, Freddie Hubbard, Curtis Fuller, Wayne Shorter, Cedar Walton, Reginald Workman, Blue Note.

155) Happy Holiday (Irving Berlin) Peggy Lee, 1965, Capitol.

156) Dear Lord (John Coltrane) Coltrane, McCoy Tyner, Roy Haynes, Jimmy Garrison, 1965. From The Original Master Tapes on Impulse Records (5 1/2"). This disc has half as many tracks as The Gentle Side of John Coltrane for a fuller sound and listening experience.

157) Song of the Jet (Samba do Aviao) (Jobim-Gene Lees) Tony Bennett, Carlos Lyra, Elcio Milito, Al Cohn, 1965. From Tony Bennett: If I Ruled the World: Songs for the Jet Set, Columbia/Sony.

158) Love Scene (Duke Ellington) Tony Bennett, 1965. From Tony Bennett: If I Ruled the World, Columbia/Sony.

159) All My Tomorrows (Sammy Cahn-Jimmy Van Heusen) Tony Bennett, Ralph Sharon, Billy Exiner, Hal Gaylor, 1965. From Tony Bennett: If I Ruled the World, Columbia/Sony. Bennett's favorite Van Heusen song.

> America in the 20s and 30s and 40s, blessed with a brotherhood of composers, experienced a renaissance of magnificent songs. Ira and George Gershwin, Jerome Kern, Cole Porter, and Irving Berlin all penned songs for Broadway shows that left the public walking on air, humming and whistling tunes that they instinctively knew would last forever. One thousand years from now, America will be adored for having created these songs.
>
> —Tony Bennett

160) For Every Man There's a Woman (Harold Arlen-Leo Robin) From Harold Sings Arlen (with friend), 1966, Columbia. Also on the compilation Harold Arlen Rediscovered. A perfect bossa nova in the style of Walter Matthew. It should be noted that Liza Minelli recorded a definitive Broadway version of this title on Liza Minelli: The Complete Capitol Collection from 1964 to 1965. Also arranged by Peter Matz. That disc includes Cole Porter's "Looking at You," in which Minelli inhabits Porter. She also rescues Arlen's affecting "I Knew Him When" from obscurity. In 1984, Paul McCartney's MPL Communications purchased the publishing rights to Arlen's songs.

161) Pedro Pedreiro (Chico Buarque) Nara Leao 1966 from Nara Pede Passagem. Universal/Japan. The muse of the bossa nova.

162) Upa Neguinho (Edu Lobo-Gianfrancesco Guarnieri) Elis Regina and Bossa Jazz Trio, 1966. From Dois Na Bossa Numero 2 Elis Regina E Jair Rodrigues. Philips/Universal.

163) Sweet Happy Life (Luiz Bonfa, Norman Gimbel) Peggy Lee 1966 from Ultimate Peggy Lee on Capitol, 2020 compilation.

164) Afinidad (Erroll Garner) Garner, Milt Hinton, Johnny Pacheco, Art Ryerson, 1966. From Erroll Garner: That's My Kick. Mack Avenue Records.

165) Mariana, Mariana (Edu Lobo-Ruy Guerra) from Edu, 1966, A Arte De Mariana Bethiana. The version that opens with cellos.

166) Image (Luiz Eca-Aloysio De Olivera-Ray Gilbert) from Sylvia Telles: The Voice I Love, 1966, El Records.

167) Discussao (Jobim-Mendonca) Sylvia Telles, Salvador da Silva, Chico Batera, Rubens Bassini, 1966. Corcovado Music Corp. From Bossa Nova Jazz Club/Highlights, Verve/Universal.

168) Sonho De Um Carnaval (Chico Buarque), 1966. Som Livre Label.

169) Candeias (Edu Lobo), 1967. From Edu Lobo, Dubas Musica. The bonus track for voice and violao, preferred over studio version, pure with torque at the outset.

170) Meu Caminho (Dori Caymmi-Edu Lobo) Edu Lobo, Dori Caymmi, Dorio Perreira, Papao, Copinha, Peter Dauelsberg. Arr: by Dori Caymmi, 1967. From Edu Lobo, Dubas Musica.

171) The Crickets Sing for Anamaria (Marcos Valle-Paulo Sergio Valle) Walter Wanderly, Sebastiao Neto, Dom Um Romao, 1967. From Walter Wanderly Orgao, Sax E Sexy + 0 Successco e Samba. A better cheddar, Wanderly was introduced to Creed Taylor by Tony Bennett. Recording forty-six albums, he was offered a dream gig with Holiday Inns to play in the US, Mexico, and Japan but became too fond of Johnnie Walker.

172) Broadway Medley: Broadway (McRae/Woode/Bird) Crazy Rhythm (Caesar/Kahn/Meyer) Lullaby of Broadway (Dubin-Warren) Tony Bennett, 1967. From For Once in My Life/I've Gotta Be Me, BGO Records. Brilliant.

173) I've Been Wrong Before (Randy Newman) Dusty Springfield. From You Don't Have to Say You Love Me, 1966, Mercury.

Mimi Rosenblum, hoofing in the 50s

Bop City, New York City, 1953
(© Herman Leonard Photography, LLC)

Billie Holiday and nephew, Los Angeles, 1953
(© Herman Leonard Photography, LLC)

Allen Toussaint
(© Barry Kaiser)

A tax meeting cocktail hour at a midtown Manhattan hotel. Accounts appreciate a good number.
(Photo by Gary Firstenberg)

Frank Sinatra, New York City, 1956
(© Herman Leonard Photography, LLC)

Buddy Rich and Oscar, Peterson, Paris, 1958
(© Herman Leonard Photography, LLC)

Major Holly, July 1959
(© Chuck Stewart Photography, LLC)

Billy Strayhorn, Paris, 1960
(© Herman Leonard Photography, LLC)

Duke Ellington, Paris, 1960
(© Herman Leonard Photography, LLC)

Peggy Lee with Tony Bennett and his wife in green room, 1962
(© Bob Gomel)

Antonio Carlos Jobim, Hollywood Hills, CA, 1964
(Photo by William Claxton, courtesy of Demont Photo Management, LLC)

Ray Charles, 1995
(© Barry Kaiser)

New Yorker *cartoon*
by Paul Noth, 2011
(Courtesy of the artist)

"You can't blame everything on the bossa nova."

Buddy Guy at Jazz Fest, 2023
(© Barry Kaiser)

An overhead shot of Jazz Fest
(© Barry Kaiser)

174) Cassandra (Dave Brubeck) Brubeck, Paul Desmond, Joe Morrello, Gene Wright, 1966. From Time In, Columbia/Legacy.

175) Don't Let Me Lose This Dream (Aretha Franklin-Ted White) Aretha Franklin, 1967, Atlantic. "More Bass"—Jerry Wexler

176) Christmas Will Really Be Christmas (J. W. Alexander/B. Raleigh) Lou Rawls, 1967, Capitol.

177) Mancada (Gilberto Gil) from Louvacao, 1967. Philips on Estrelas Brasilieras.

178) Feitnha Pro Poeta (Baden Powell) Baden Powell, 1967. From Poema on Guitar: Baden Powell, MPS Records/Japanese Import.

179) All the Things You Are (Jerome Kern) Baden Powell, 1967. From Poema on Guitar: Baden Powell, MPS Records/Japanese Import.

180) Stay (Gayle Caldwell) Astrud Gilberto, Ron Carter, Hubert laws, Bobby Rosengarden, Grady Tate, 1967. From Beach Samba, Verve.

181) Baubles, Bangles, and Beads (Forrest-Wright-Borodin) Sinatra/Jobim, 1967/2010 remastering. Universal. Arr: Claus Ogerman.

182) Why Don't They Know (Roland Kirk) Kirk, Lonnie Smith, Grady Tate, 1967, Emarcy.

183) Vivo Sonhando (Jobim) Luiz Henrique, 1967. From Jazz Samba, Verve. Groovy.

184) She's a Carioca (Jobim) Stanley Turrentine, Donald Byrd, Joe Farrell, Bucky Pizzarelli, Pepper Adams, Ron Carter, Blue Mitchell, Mickey Roker, Kenny Barron, Jerry Dodgion, Julian Priester. Arr: Duke Pearson, 1967. From A Bluish Bag, Blue Note. Bucky digs in.

185) Samba Do Aviao (Jobim) Stanley Turrentine et al from A Bluish Bag, 1967, Blue Note.

186) Catavento (Milton Nascimento) Milton, Danilo Caymmi, Luiz Eca, Dorio Ferreira. From Bossa Nova Lounge/Dreamer, 1967, Dubas Musica.

187, 188, 189, 190, 191) Look to the Sky, Batidinha, Triste, Mojave, Lamento (Jobim) (Jobim-DeMoraes) from Wave, 1967. A&M Jasrac/Japanese import (red cover) Antonio Carlos Jobim, Jimmy Cleveland, Urbie Green, Ray Beckenstein, Romeo Penque, Jerome Richardson, Ron Carter, Dom Um Romao, Bobby Rosengarden, Claudio Slon. Arr: Claus Ogerman. Ron Carter dances more clearly on the red cover import.

192) Candeias (Edu Lobo) from Edu Lobo Novo Millenium/Universal. Vocalist unnamed, Likely Gal Costa, 1967.

193) Ain't No Way (Carolyn Franklin) from The Genius of Aretha Franklin, 1968/2020, Atlantic/Rhino.

194) Speak Like a Child (Herbie Hancock) Hancock, Ron Carter, Mickey Roker, Thad Jones, Jerry Dodgion, 1968. From Speak Like a Child, Blue Note. Sounds like a Boeing 747.

195) Easy Street (A.R. Jones) Thelonious Monk, Larry Gales, Ben Riley, 1968. From Thelonious Monk: Underground. Columbia. Produced by Teo Macero.

196) Cancao Da Terra (Edu Lobo-Vincius De Moraes) Edu Lobo, 1968. From Com A Participacoa Do Tamba Trio. Elenco.

197) A Bientot (Billy Taylor) Freddie Hubbard, Bennie Maupin, James Spaulding, Howard Johnson, Kenny Barron, Louis Hayes. From High Pressure Blues, 1968, Koch Jazz/Atlantic.

198) Tema Para Morte e Vida Severina (Chico Buarque) Chico Buarque De Hollanda Vol. 3, 1968, Som Livre.

199) Nica's Dream (Horace Silver) Oscar Peterson, Sam Jones, Bobby Durham, 1968. From Exclusively for My Friends, MPS/Verve.

200) Punky's Dilemma (Paul Simon) Paul Simon and Art Garfunkel, 1968. From Bookends, Columbia/Legacy.

201) Punky's Dilemma (Paul Simon) Barbra Streisand, 1969. From What About Today? Arr: Peter Matz. Columbia.

202) South American Getaway (Burt Bacharach) from Butch Cassidy and the

Sundance Kid soundtrack, 1969, A&M. Bacharach named Jobim and Milton Nascimento among his greatest influences.

203) This Happy Madness (Estrada Branca) (Jobim-Lee-DeMoraes) Sinatra/Jobim, 1969/2010, remastering on Concord. From Sinatra/Jobim: The Complete Reprise Recordings. Arr: Eumir Deodato

204) Bonita (Gilbert-Jobim- Lees) Sinatra/Jobim, 1969/2010 remastering on Concord. From Sinatra/Jobim: The Complete Reprise Recordings. Arr: Eumir Deodato. Inspired by a young Candice Bergen, introduced to Tom at Nesuhi Ertegun's home.

205) Morro Velho (Milton Nascimento) Milton, Herbie Hancok, Airto, Hubert Laws, Charles McCracken, Wayne Andre, Romeo Penque, Jerome Richardson, Marvin Stamm, Bill Watrous. From Courage, 1969, A&M. Arr: Emir Deodato.

206) From the Hot Afternoon (Milton Nascimento) Paul Desmond, Dorio Ferreira, Ron Carter, Airto Moreira, 1969, A&M/Verve. Alternate take track #13 3:40."

207) Lazy Afternoon (John Latouche-Jerome Moross) Joe Henderson, Herbie Hancock, Ron Carter, and Jack DeJohnette, 1969. From Joe Henderson: Power to the People. Keepnews Collection.

208) Ramblin' (Maybelle Smith) Aretha Franklin. From Soul '69, Atlantic. Arr: Arif Mardin.

209) Ugetsu (Cedar Walton) Cedar Walton, Bob Cranshaw, Mickey Roker, 1969, Prestige. From Cedar Walton Plays Cedar Walton. Ear candy.

210) California, Here I Come (Meyer-Jolson-Ballantine-DeSylva) Bill Evans, Eddie Gomez, Marty Morell, 1969. From Bill Evans: Jazzhouse, Milestone Records "Right back where I started from."

211) Sleepin' Bee (Harold Arlen-Truman Capote) Bill Evans, Eddie Gomez, Marty Morell, 1969. From Bill Evans: Jazzhouse, Milestone. There is a mesmerizing video of this on Bill Evans Jazz Icons DVD.

212) Samba E Amor (Chico Buarque De Hollanda) from Chico Buarque, 1970, Philips/Universal.

213) Pois E (So It Is) (A.C. Jobim-Chico Buarque) from Chico Revisited, 1970, Dubas Musica.

214) Falsa Baiana (Geraldo Pereira) Gal Costa, 1970. From Gal Costa: Legal, Philips.

215) Come for a Dream (Jobim-Dolores Duran-Norma Tanega) Dusty Springfield, 1970. From Come for a Dream: the UK sessions, Atlantic/Rhino.

216) Marta E Romao (Edu Lobo-Gianfrancesco Guarnieri) from Edu Lobo-Cantiga De Longe, 1970, Elenco/Universal/Emarcy.

217, 218) Garota De Ipanema, Se Todos Fosem Iguais a Voce (Jobim-Vinicius) from Vinicius De Moraes con Maria Creuza, Maria Bethiana y Toquinho, 1970, Disc Medi. The last and first songs written by Jobim/DeMoraes.

219) Tarde Em Itapoa (Toquinho-Vinicius) from Vinicius de Moraes con Maria Creuza etc. 1971, Disc Medi.

220) Apelo (Baden Powell-Vinicius) from Vinicius de Moraes con Maria Creuza et al, 1971, Disc Medi.

221) Comanche (Jorge Ben) from Jorge Ben: Negro e Lindo. Phonogram/Philips/Universal. Also on Black Rio. Strut Records, 1971.

222) Eu O Crepuscolo (Johnny Alf) from Bossa Nova Lounge: Dreamer on Dubas Musica, 1971. Originally from Ele e Johnny Alf. EMI. Muito bonito.

223) Essa Passou (Carlos Lyra-Chico Buarque) Carlos Lyra and Chico Buarque, 1971. From Tropique Samba Lounge: Samba E Amor, Dubas Musica.

224) Ponteio (Edu Lobo-Capinam) Astrud Gilberto, Toots Thielmans, Stanley Turrentine, 1971, CTI Arr; Eumir Deodato.

225) Salt Song (Milton Nascimento) Stanley Turrentine, Ron Carter, Richard Tee, Jerome Richardson, Hubert Laws, Airto Moreira, 1971. Arr: Eumir Deodato, CTI. Mr. T quotes Harry Warren nicely.

226) Tereza Da Praia (Jobim-Billy Blanco) Dick Farney with Lucio Alves,

1971. From Meus Momentos: Dick Farney, EMI. Not to be confused with Teresa Da Praia (Tereza of the Beach) recorded in 1954.

227) Sugar Plum (Bill Evans) from The Bill Evans Album, Columbia/Legacy, 1971, with Eddie Gomez and Marty Morell.

228) Nite Life (Mary Lou Williams) from Mary Lou Williams: Nite Life, 1971, Chiarascuro. "Originally recorded forty-one years before on April 24, 1930, and always referred to by Mary Lou Williams as my first record." One hears the influence of James P. Johnson and Earl Hines—Peter F. O'Brien, S. J.

229) Three Little Words (Bert Kalmar and Harry Ruby) Carmen McRae, Jimmy Rowles, Joe Pass, Chuck Domenico, and Chuck Flores, 1971. From Carmen McRae: The Great American Songbook. Atlantic. This double vinyl recording has been compressed into a single CD, which, while passable, is not the revelation that the original non-compressed recording is. Finding a double CD on East West Japan was my reward for a lifetime of poring over dusty bins on the floor. The original is available at this typing on vinyl and would recommend hearing Jimmy Rowles in his full glory, on a discrete track.

230) Immigration Man (Graham Nash) from Graham Nash/David Crosby, 1971, Atlantic/Rhino. Nash grew up just outside Manchester; he became a US citizen in the early eighties. Timely.

231) Simon Smith and the Dancing Bear (Randy Newman) From Sail Away, 1972, Warner Brothers.

232) I Think I Can Hear You (Carole King) from Rhymes and Reasons, 1972, Epic.

233) A Felicidade (Jobim-DeMoraes) Maria Creuza, Toqhinho, and Vinicius De Moraes, 1972, Disc Medi.

234) Enlouqueci (Luiz Soberana/Joao Salles/Waldomiro Pereira dos Santos) Alaide Costa, Milton Nascimento, Luiz Eca, 1972. From Tropique Samba Lounge: Samba e Amor. Dubas Musica.

235) Izaura (Herivelto Martino-Roberto Roberti) Joao Gilberto and Miucha. From Joao Gilberto (white album), Polydor, 1973, also on Universal/Japan for pure clarity. SANS Stan Getz.

236) Music (Carole King) from Carole King Music, 1973, Ode. Curtis Amy, saxophone.

237) Little Trip to Heaven (Tom Waits) from Closing Time, 1973, Anti/Epitath.

238) Tenderness (Paul Simon) Simon, Cornell Dupre, Rick Marotta, Dixie Hummingbirds. From There Goes Rhymin' Simon, 1973, Columbia. Horn Arr: Allen Toussaint.

239) Summertime (Gershwins) Oscar Peterson in Russia, 1974, Pablo records.

240) Bonita (Jobim, Ray Gilbert, Gene Lees) Elis Regina, Oscar Castro-Neves, Luizao Maia, Paulo Braga, 1974. From Antonio Carlos Jobim: The Man from Ipanema. On Jazz Heritage/Verve/Polygram.

241) Ligia (Tom Jobim) Chico Buarque, 1974. From Sem Limite Series. Mercury/Universal.

242) Free Cell Block F, Tis Nazi USA (Charles Mingus) Mingus, George Adams, Don Pullen, Dannie Richmond. From Changes Two, 1974, Atlantic.

243) Voce (Roberto Menescal-Ronaldo Boscoli) Dick Farney and Claudette Soares. From The Bossa Nova Wave, 1974/2001, EMI.

244) Feio Nao e Bonito (Carlos Lyra-Gianfrancesco Guarnieri) Carlos Lyra, 1974, Discobertas. Warner Music Brazil.

245) In the Name of Love (Estelle Levitt/Kenny Rankin) from The Best of Kenny Rankin, 1974, Peaceful/Rhino Records.

246) The Touch of Your Lips (Ray Noble) (take one) Tony Bennett and Bill Evans, 1975. From The Complete Recordings, Fantasy/Concord. This is the alternate take with piano intro.

> Ray Noble, whose band played in the United States during the thirties, wrote only a few songs, but all of them were very good. Insofar as he is not an American, it might be suggested that his songs don't belong in this summary. Yet his songs are so American in style and so loved by Americans that he is musically American by adoption. I doubt that most of those who like his songs know that they were written by an Englishman.
>
> —Alec Wilder

247) Exuberante (Arturo O'Farrill) Dizzy Gillespie, Victor Paz, Raul Gonzalez, Ramon Gonzalez Jr., Manny Duran, Barry Morrow, Jack Jeffers, Lewis Kahn, Jerry Chamberlin, Mario Bauza, Mauicio Smith, Jose Madera Sr., Leslie Yahonikan, Mario Rivera, Carlos Castillo, Jorge Dalto, Julito Collazo, R. Hernandez, Mario Grillo, Pepin Pepin, Jose Madera Jr., Mickey Roker, Dana McCurdy. Arranged and conducted by Chico O'Farrill, 1975. From Gillespie Y Machito: Afro-Cuban Jazz Moods, Pablo Records.

248) Don't Let No One Get You Down (D. Allen/H. Brown/B.B Dickerson/L. Jordan/C. Miller/L. Oskar/H. Scott/J. Goldstein) War, 1975. From Why Can't We Be Friends? Also on War/The Hits and More. ICON 2/Hip-O Records/ Far Out Productions/Universal.

249) Once I Loved (Jobim) McCoy Tyner, Ron Carter, Elvin Jones, 1975. From Trident, Milestone Records. Like Coltrane meets bossa nova.

250) Catalonian Nights (Dexter Gordon) Gordon, Tete Montoliu, Niels-Henning Orsted Pederson, Billy Higgins, 1975. From Bouncin' with Dex, Steeplechase. This sounds more like Montoliu's writing, but no matter. Montoliu at the time was the greatest jazz musician to come out of Spain.

251) Since We Met (Bill Evans) from Bill Evans: Alone (again), 1975, Fantasy. This beautiful track is not on the original US release; I discovered it by accident. Not to be confused with the trio version from 1974 at the Village Vanguard, this is a solo, a more polished and concise version that reminds me a bit of Chopin/Scarlatti. JASRAC/Victor/Tokyo. If it weren't worth the time, trouble, and expense to piano/Bill Evans lovers, it wouldn't be on the list.

252) Bluebird (Leon Russell) Leon Russell, Teddy Jack Eddy, Mary McCreary, Patrick Henderson, 1975. From Will o' The Wisp The Right Stuff Label.

253) Rainbow in Your Eyes (Leon Russell) Leon and Mary Russell and Teddy Jack Eddy, 1976. From Leon and Mary Russell: Wedding Album, Wounded Bird Records.

254) I Want You (Leon Ware) Marvin Gaye, 1976, Motown (also Gato Barbieri on Calliente!).

255) Dark Cloud (Zoot Sims) Zoot Sims, Oscar Brashear, Snooky Young, Frank

Rosolino, Richie Kamuca, Jerome Richardson, Ross Tompkins, Monty Bundwig, Nick Ceroli. From Hawthorne Nights, 1976. Arr: Bill Holman. OJC/Fantasy.

256) Sweet Talk (Cy Coleman-Carolyn Leigh) Mabel Mercer, Loonis McGlohon, Terry Lassiter, Jim Lackey, 1976. From Mabel Mercer: Echoes of Life, Audiophile.

257) How Little We Know (Hoagy Carmichael-Johnny Mercer) Susannah McCorkle & Co. 1977. From The Classic Hoagy Carmichael/The Indiana Historical Society. The audio is superior to original Jazz Alliance disc on Concord. Perhaps Concord will remaster in a compilation. Also in the 1944 film "To Have and Have Not," Lauren Bacall and Hoagy Carmichael perform a delightful version of this title.

258) Buckaroo (Bob Morris) from Leo Kotke, 1977, Chrysalis/BGO Records.

259) Racetrack in France (Brian Jackson-Gil Scott-Heron) from Gil Scot-Heron and Brian Jackson, 1977, Anthology/Messages, Arista.

260) Flor D' Luna (Moonflower) (Tom Coster) Santana, 1977. From Moonflower, Columbia/Legacy.

261) Fair Game (Stephen Stills) Crosby, Stills, Nash & Ray Baretto, 1977. From CSN, Atlantic.

262) Down in Brazil (Michael Franks) Franks, Joao Donato, 1977. From Michael Franks, Sleeping Gypsy.

263) I Wish It Were Yesterday (R.L. Martin/L. Phillips) Lou Rawls, 1977. From When You Hear Lou, You've Heard It All. Produced and arranged by Billy Martin (what a Renaissance man!) Philadelphia Intl Records/Sony/BMG/Legacy.

264) Don't Worry 'Bout Me (T. Koehler-R. Bloom) Dave Brubeck, Paul Desmond, Joe Morello, Eugene Wright, 1977. From The Dave Brubeck Quartet/25th Annual Reunion A&M,

265) Dream Dancing (Cole Porter) Zoot Sims, Jimmy Rowles, George Mraz, Mousey Alexander, 1978. From Warm Tenor, Pablo Records.

266) Sno' Peas (Phil Markowitz) Bill Evans, Toots Thielmans, Marc Johnson, Eliot Zigmund, Larry Schneider. Recorded by Frank Laico. Produced by Helen Keane, 1978. From Bill Evans/Toots Thielmans: Affinity. Warner Bros.

267) I Love My Wife (Cy Coleman, Michael Stewart) Bill Evans from New Conversations, 1978. Warner Bros. Evans' fellow New Jerseyan Frank Sinatra sang/recorded this song affectingly.

268) New Dance (Keith Jarrett) Jarrett, Jan Garbarek, Palle Danielsson, Jon Christensen, 1979 at the Village Vanguard. From Keith Jarrett: Nude Ants. ECM.

269) The Search (Pat Metheny, Lyle Mays) Metheny, Mays, Mark Egan, and Dan Gottlieb, 1979. From Pat Matheney Group: American Garage on ECM.

270) Amargua (Radames Gnatalli/Alberto Ribeiro) Nana Caymmi, 1979, on Nana Caymmi: 2 em 1, EMI.

271) Ai Quem Me Dera (Tom Jobim-Marino Pinto) Quarteto em Cy, 1981. From Quarteto em Cy: Cy: Caminhos Cruzados, RGE.

272) Sanfona (Egberto Gismonti) Gismonti, Zeca Assumpcao, Mauro Senise, 1981. From Em Familia; also on Antologia/Egberto Gismonti, EMI. Not as readily accessible on album titled Sanfona.

273) Pretty Libby (Mac Rebennack), 1982. From Dr. John Plays Mac Rebennack: The Legendary Sessions, Volume Two. Cleancutsmusic.

274) Brazil (Ary Barroso-S.K. Russell) Barney Kessel. From Barney Kessel: Solo, 1983, Concord.

275) Solidao (Jobim-A Fernandes) Dick Farney, 1986. From No Palco! Musica Brasileira. "The epitome of sophistication is utter simplicity"—Maya Angelou

276) Coracao Vagabundo (Caetano Veloso) from Caetano Veloso: The Definitive Collection, 1986, Wrasse Records. On this compilation, the song has more presence and weight than the original Nonesuch recording.

277) Mine (Gershwins) from Manhattan Soundtrack, 1987. Dick Hyman, Milt Hinton. Sony (Everybody Loves Raymond).

278) Now It Can Be Told (Irving Berlin) Tony Bennett and the Ralph Sharon Trio, 1987, Columbia. From Bennett/Berlin. "Lyrical in a way new to Berlin"—Alec Wilder. Wrapped up in the movie "It Could Happen to You," starring Nicholas Cage and Rosie Perez, Hollywood with a saxophone.

279) Passarim (Tom Jobim) Tom Jobim e a nova banda, 1987. From the compilation "MPB," Mercury/Universal. This compilation has the Portuguese version with superior sound to the original; the needle engages more fully with the groove. Strong musically and ecologically.
   "Is it possible to be more sophisticated than Tom Jobim?"—Edu Lobo

280) Suddenly (live) (Thelonious Monk-Jon Hendricks) instrumentally known as In Walked Bud; Louise (Richard Whiting-Leo Robin) Carmen McRae, Larry Willis, Charlie Rouse, Al Foster, George Mraz, 1988, BMG/RCA from Carmen Sings Monk. "Every little breeze seems to whisper Louise"—Leo Robin

281) Once I Loved (Antonio Carlos Jobim/Vinicius DeMoraes/Ray Gilbert) Shirley Horn, Charles Ables, Steve Williams, 1988. From Shirley Horn: Close Enough for Love, Verve. Sublime.

282) Chovenda Na Roseira (ACJ) Paulo Jobim, Gilson Peranzetta, Tiao Neto, Paulo Braga, Danilo Caymmi, Jacques Morelenbaum, Simone Caymmi, Elizabeth Jobim, Eveline Hecker, 1989. From Familia Jobim. Movie Play Records. A beautiful double rainbow.

283) East of the Sun (West of the Moon) (Brooks Bowman) Marcus Roberts, Reginald Veal, Herlin Riley, 1987-90. From Wynton Marsalis Standard Time Vol. 2, Intimacy Calling, Columbia.

284) I Cover the Waterfront (J. Green-E Heyman) Wynton Marsalis, Ellis Marsalis, Reginald Veal, and Herlin Riley, 1990. From Wynton Marsalis Standard Time Vol. 3, The Resolution of Romance, Columbia. (See Louis' I Cover in Ken Burns' Jazz). Experience Ellis.

285) Sem Compromisso (Geraldo Pereira/Nelson Trigueira) Joao Gilberto Live in Montreux, 1990, Rhino/Elektra. A swinging pure samba, without compromise.

286) Pedro Pedreiro (Chico Buarque) From Chico em Cy, 1991, CID.

287) Song of the Jet (Jobim) Joyce Breach, Lonis McGlohon, Joe Negri, Virgil Walters, and Reid Hoyson, 1991. From Confessions, Audiophile Records.

288) O Orvalho Vem Caindo (Noel Rosa/Kid Pepe) Carlos Lyra and Veronica Sabino, 1991. From Songbook Noel on Lumiar; Lumiar Colecao Songbook Vol. 4.

289) Quando O Samba Acabou (Noel Rosa) Leila Pinheiro and Roberto Menescal, 1991. From Songbook Noel on Lumiar.

290) Meu Barracao (Noel Rosa) Caetano Veloso and Marcello Costa, 1991. From Songbook Noel on Lumiar.

291) Errinho A Toa (Roberto Menescal-Ronaldo Boscoli) Leila Pinheiro and Roberto Menescal, 1991. From A Bossa De Leila Pinheiro, Universal/Mercury.

292) Call Me (E So Chamar) (Tony Hatch-Nelson Motta) Leila Pinheiro and Roberto Menescal, 1991. From A Bossa De Leila Pinheiro, Universal/Mercury.

293) Nancy (Phil Silvers-Jimmy Van Heusen) Tony Bennett and the Ralph Sharon Trio, 1992. From Perfectly Frank, Columbia. "Summer could take some lessons from her."—Phil Silvers

294) Last Night When We Were Young (Harold Arlen-Yip Harburg) Tony Bennett and the Ralph Sharon Trio, 1992, Columbia. From Perfectly Frank. Sinatra and Bennett recorded three masterpieces of this title. This is the fourth, the one that swings, with no strings attached. Arlen's hero, George Gershwin, told his younger colleague that the song went on too long. "Harold Arlen was my very favorite . . . Yip Harburg."—Tony Bennett

295) This Is It (Arthur Schwartz-Dorothy Fields) KT Sullivan, Mike Renzi, Tony Leonhardt, Dave Ratjczak, 1992. From Arthur Schwartz: Smithsonian Collection of Recordings/DRG.

296) How Am I to Know? (Jack King-Dorothy Parker) Shirley Horn, Charles Ables, Steve Williams, James Walker. Arr: Johnny Mandel, 1992. From Shirley Horn: Here's to Life, Verve.

297) Piano Na Mangueira (Tom Jobim-Chico Buarque) Buarque, Jobim, Luiz Claudio Ramos, Luizao, Wilson das Neves, Roberto Marques. Arr: Tom

Jobim, 1992. From Paratodos by Chico Buarque, BMG/RCA.

298) Zingaro (Jobim) George Shearing Trio. From I Hear a Rhapsody: Live at the Blue Note, 1992, Telarc. Also known as Portrait in Black and White.

299) Speak Low (Kurt Weill-Ogden Nash) Diane Schur, Dori Caymmi, Roger Kellaway, Tom Scott, Chuck Domenico, and Will Kennedy. From Diane Schur: Love Songs, 1993, GRP. Believe composer wrote this "weill" in the US.

300) I Guess I'll Have to Change My Plan (Schwartz-Dietz) Tony Bennett and the Ralph Sharon Trio, 1993. From Steppin' Out, Columbia. The exclamatory intro is Fred Astaire's exact arrangement, only with Bennett, Sharon's Trio, and a clearer, fuller recording. Disc briefly makes an appearance in the movie, analyze this.

301) It Only Happens When I Dance With You (Irving Berlin) Tony Bennett and the Ralph Sharon Trio, 1993. From Steppin' Out, Columbia. A bullseye to the heart.

302) Shine on Your Shoes (Schwartz-Dietz) Tony Bennett and the Ralph Sharon Trio, 1993. From Steppin' Out, Columbia.

303) Trouble Is a Man (Alec Wilder) Marian McPartland Trio, 1993, Concord. Beautiful.

304) Heat Wave (Irving Berlin) Mario Bauza and the Afro-Cuban orchestra. From Mario Bauza and he Afro-Cuban Orchestra/944 Columbus. Messidor. Recorded May 1993 in NYC. Bauza died in July 1993 in the apt at 944 Columbus Avenue, where he lived for half a century. Arr: Ray Santos.

305) Antigua (Antonio Carlos Jobim) Ken Peplowski, Ben Aronov, Alan Dawson, Howard Alden, John Goldsby, 1993, Concord Jazz. From Ken Peplowski & Friends.

306) O Bem Do Mar (Dorival Caymmi) Tom Jobim and Ana Jobim. From Dorival Caymmi Songbook, 1993, Lumiar Discos/Sony Music.

307) Tennessee Stud (Jimmy Driftwood) Johnny Cash, 1994, American Recordings.

308) Wanton Spirit (Earl McDonald) Kenny Barron, Charlie Haden, Roy Haynes, 1994. From Wanton Spirit, Verve.

309) Threnody (Marian McPartland) from Marian McPartland Plays the Music of Mary Lou Williams, 1994, Concord.

310) Swing Low, Sweet Chariot (public domain) Charlie Haden and Hank Jones, 1994. From Steal Away, Verve.

311) Surfboard (Jobim, musica) Tom Jobim, Paulo Jobim, Sebastiao Neto, Paulo Braga, Jacques Morelenbaum, Danilo Caymmi, Ana Jobim, Elizabeth Jobim, Maucha Adnet, Paula Morelenbaum, Simone Caymmi, Marcio Montarroyos, Edeneck Svab, and Antonio Jose Augusto, 1994. From Antonio Brasiliero, Sony.

312) I Was Just One More for You (Jobim-Billy Blanco) from Salena Jones Sings with the Jobims, 1994, (also see YouTube video under this song title/ Salena Jones). Hopefully, Lumiar will reissue this beautiful composition one day. It is also known as Esperanza by Jane Duboc, Cristavao Bastos, and Vittor Santos.

313) Eu Vim Da Bahia (Gilberto Gil) Gilberto Gil, 1994. From Elis Regina No Fino Bossa, Velas.

314) Cartao De Visita (Calling Card) (Carlos Lyra/Vinicius DeMoraes) Wanda Sa and Roberto Menescal, 1994. From Songbook Vinicius De Moraes 2 on Lumiar; also on Colecao Songbook Vol. 4 on Lumiar.

315) Na Batucada Da Vida (Ary Barroso/Luiz Peixoto) Antonio Carlos Jobim, Paulo Jobim, Paulo Braga, Tiao Neto, Vittor Santos, 1994. From Songbook Ary Barroso Vol. 1 on Lumiar.

316) Maria (Ary Barroso/Luiz Peixoto) Edu Lobo, Cristavao Bastos, Nelson Faria, Adriano Giffoni, Nilton Rodrigues, Dirceu Leite, Lura Ranevsky, Robertinho Silva, and Firmino, 1994. From Songbook Ary Barroso Vol. 1, Lumiar.

317) Para Machuar Meu Coracao (Ary Barroso) Edu Lobo, Antonio Carlos Jobim, Paulo Jobim, Tiao Neto, Paulo Braga, 1994. From Songbook Ary Barroso Vol. 2, Lumiar.

318) Coisa Do Carnaval (Ary Barroso) Johnny Alf, Cristavao Bastos, Joao Lilra, Marcos Souza, Ramon Montanhaur, Idriss Boudrioua, Chacal, 1994. From Songbook Ary Barroso Vol. 3, Lumiar.

319) Malandro Sofredor (Ary Barroso) Carlinhos Vergueiro, Vittor Santos, Lula Galvao, Ricardo Amado, Wilson da Neves, Adriano Giffoni, Trambique, 1994. From Songbook Vol. 3, Lumiar.

320) Estrada Do Sol (Jobim/Dolores Duran) Nana Caymmi, Dori Caymmi, Cristavao Bastos, Jorge Helder, Ricardo Costa, 1994. From Nana Caymmi (album) and A Noite Do Meu Bem (CD), EMI.

321) Key Largo (Benny Carter, Karl Sussedorf, and Leah Worth) Carmen Bradford, Benny Carter, Chris Neville, Steve Laspina, Roy McCurdy, 1995. From The Benny Carter Songbook, Musicmasters Jazz.

322) Garota De Ipanema (Jobim-De Moraes) Lisa Ono and Joao Donato, 1995. From Heirs to Jobim, RCA/BMG.

323) Wild Man Blues (Louis Armstrong-Jelly Roll Morton) Nicholas Payton, Antony Wonsey, Reuben Rogers, Adonis Rose, 1995. From Nicholas Payton: Gumbo Nouveau, Verve.

324) Mandinga (Rodriguez Fiffe) Ruben Gonzalez, piano; Amadito Valdes, timbales; Roberto Garcia, bongos; Carlos Gonzalez, congas; Orlando "Cachaito" Lopez, bass; Guajiro Mirabal, trumpet, 1997. From Introducing Ruben Gonzalez, World Circuit.

325) Walking My Baby Back Home (Fred Ahlert-Roy Turk) James Taylor. From Hourglass, 1997, Columbia.

326) Some Other Spring (Arthur Herzog Jr.-Irene Kitchings) Tony Bennett, Ralph Sharon. Arr: Jorge Calandrelli, 1997. From Tony Bennett on Holiday, Columbia. Art Tatum's Trio recorded this on Pablo, swinging like a warm knife through butter. Bennett's version has more depth.

327) I See Your Face Before Me (Schwartz-Dietz) Kevin Mahogany, Roy Hargrove, Barry Harris, Christian McBride, T.S. Monk Jr. from Eastwood After Hours/Live at Carnegie Hall 1997 Malpaso/Warner Bros. Records

328) Brigas Nunca Mais (Jobim) Elliane Elias and Oscar Castro-Neves, 1997. From The Three Americas, Blue Note. Impeccable.

329) Choro Bandido (Edu Lobo-Chico Buarque) Edu and Tom Jobim and Jacques Morelenbaum. From De Teatro: Edu Lobo and Chico Buarque, 1997. BMG/MP3. MP3 only at this typing. This title has been recorded in a number of musical combinations. To my ears, this is the richest.

330) Passa Por Mim (Marcos Valle/Paulo Sergio Valle) Nana Caymmi, Cristavao Bastos, Joao Lyra, Jorge Helder, Wilson das Neves, Paulinho Trompete, 1997-98. From songbook Marcos Valle Vol. 1, Lumiar.

331) Ao Amigo Tom (Marcos Valle, Paulo Sergio Valle, and Osmar Milito) Emilio Santiago, Leandro Braga, Joao Lyra, Jose Pienasola, Wilson das Neves, Zero, Chico Sa, 1997-98. From Songbook Marcos Valle Vol. 1, Lumiar.

332) Festival in Bahia (McCoy Tyner) McCoy Tyner, Gary Bartz, Claudio Roditi, Steve Turre, Ignacio Berroa, Dave Valentin, Avery Sharpe, Johnny Almendra, and Giovanni Hidalgo, 1998. From McCoy Tyner and the Latin All-Stars, Telarc.

333) Por Favor (Ivan Lins/Adir Blanc) Leila Pinheiro. From BIS: Leila Pinheiro, 1998, EMI.

334) Swinging on a Star (J. Van Heusen-J. Burke) Tony Bennett and the Ralph Sharon Trio, 1998. From Tony Bennett: The Playground, Columbia. Jimmy Van Heusen was a WWII test pilot by day and Sinatra's in-house composer by afternoon and drinking buddy/personal pilot by night. He is buried in the Sinatra family plot in California. His tombstone is inscribed Swinging on a Star.

335) La Vem a Baiana (Dorival Caymmi) Jussara Silveira from Dorival Caymmi/Sem limite 1998 Universal

336) Pois E (Jobim-Buarque) Os Cariocas, Cristavao Bastos, Joao Lyra, Jorge Helder, Marcos Amma Ricardo Pontes, Joao Cortez, 1999. From Chico Buarque Songbook 4, Lumiar.

337) Nicanor (Chico Buarque) Ze Renato, Ricardo Silveira, Andre Rodrigues,

Robertinho Silva, 1999. From Chico Buarque Songbook 4, Lumiar. Silveira swings sublimely.

338) Flaming Sword (Ellington) Dr. John, 1999. From Duke Elegant, Parlophone.

339) I Concentrate on You (Cole Porter) Rosemary Clooney, Oscar Castro-Neves and Paulinho da Costa, 1999. From Rosemary Clooney: Brazil, Concord Jazz. I believe this was Clooney's last recording.

340) Eu E O Meu Amor/Lamento No Morro (A.C. Jobim/Vinicius De Moraes) Paula and Jacques Morelenbaum, Daniel and Paulo Jobim, 1999. From Quarteto Jobim-Morelenbaum, Universal Music do Brasil.

341) Samba E Amor (Chico Buarque) Bebel Gilberto and Celso Fonseca, 2000, Ziriguiboom/Six Degree Records.

342) Voce Vai Ver (Jobim) Joao Gilberto, 2000. From Joao Voz E Violao, Verve. Intimate. Hopefully, Lumiar will one day reissue Emilio Santiago's great version from The Jobim Songbook.

343) Os Olhos Da Madrugada (Carlos Lyra), Adriana Giffoni, Ricardo Costa, 2000. From Carlos Lyra: Sambalanco. Rip Curl Recordings, JASRAC/Japan. *Maravilloso!*

344) I'll Never Be the Same (Signorelli-Malneck) Nicholas Payton, Peter Bernsein, Christian McBride, 2001. From Nicholas Payton: Dear Louis, Verve.

345) When the Sun Comes Out (Harold Arlen-Ted Koehler) Kenny Rankin, David Spinozza, Christian McBride, Lewis Nash, and Chris Potter, 2002. From A Song for You, Verve. Produced by Tommy LiPuma and Al Schmitt. "Love is funny, it's not always peaches, cream, and honey." Regards to Streisand.

346) She's a Carioca (Ela E Carioca) (Jobim-DeMoraes-Ray Gilbert) Celso Fonseca, Cibelle, 2002. From Celso Fonseca: Natural, Ziriguiboom/Universal. Lean and lovely.

347) Domingo Azul Do Mar (ACJ-Newton Mendonca) Wanda, Roberto Menescal, Gilson Peranzetta, Adriano Giffoni, Marcio Bahia. From Wave E O Mar, 2002, Dubas Musica.

348) Meditation (Jobim-Mendonca) Bobby Hackett, Vic Dickenson, and Dave McKenna, 2002. From Live at the Roosevelt Grill, Chiarascuro Records.

349) Eu Nao Existo Sem Voce (there is no me, unless you are near) (Jobim-De Moraes) Luciana Souza and Walter Santos, 2002. From Brazilian Duos, Sunnyside Records.

350) Alice (Tom Waits-Kathleen Brennan) Tom Waits, 2002. From Alice, Anti/Epitaph.

351) S'Wonderful (Gershwins) Diana Krall, Live in Paris, 2002, Verve.

352) I'll Be Home for Christmas (Gannon-Kent-Ram) Dianne Reeves, Peter Martins, Romero Lubambo. From Christmas Time Is Here, 2004, Blue Note.

353) Love Me (Victor Young and Ned Washington) Dick Hyman, 2004. From the soundtrack to Melinda et Melinda on Milan.

354) So Em Teus Bracos (Jobim) Nana Caymmi, 2005. From A Night in Brazil, BMG.

355) Tipitina and Me (Roy Bird/Allen Toussaint) Allen Toussaint, 2005. From Our New Orleans. Nonesuch Records. Friend/collaborator Elvis Costello spent an entire page enthusing over this track in his memoir, Unfaithful Music and Disappearing Ink.

356) Alone Together (Schwartz-Dietz) Carly Simon, 2005. From Moonlight Serenade, Columbia.

357) Nos e o mar (Menescal-Boscoli) Claudette Soares. From E Sal, E Sol, E Sul on Albatroz Music label.

358) Rio (Menescal/Boscoli) from E Sal, E Sol, E Sul, 2006. Albatroz. So Rio.

359) Quiet Nights of Quiet Stars (Jobim-Gene Lees) Queen Latifah, Oscar Castro-Neves, Toots Thielmans, 2007. From Travelin' Light, Verve.

360) Meditacao (Jobim-Mendonca) Paulo Jobim, Daniel Jobim, 2007, MP3. Produced by Robert Menescal. Can be found under Paulo Jobim/Meditacao.

From Se Todos Fossem Iguais A Voce/Homenagem A Tom Jobim, if still in print. Beautifully spare.

361) So Tinha De Ser Com Voce (Jobim-Aloysio de Oliveira) Corcovado Music Corp. Karrin Allyson, vocal; Rod Feeman, acoustic guitars; David Finck, acoustic bass; Todd Strait, drums; Michael Spiro, shaker, 2007. On Karrin Allyson/Imagina: Songs of Brazil. Airtight; nice photos.

362) A Primeira Vez (Bide-Armando Marcal) Jane Monheit and Romero Lubambo, 2008. From The Lovers, the Dreamers, and Me, Concord.

363) Este Seu Olhar (Antonio Carlos Jobim) Diana Krall, Paulinho Da Costa, Claus Ogerman, Al Schmitt, Tommy LiPuma, 2009. From Diana Krall: Quiet Nights, Verve.

364) Baltimore (Randy Newman) 2011. From The Randy Newman Songbook Vol. 2, Nonesuch. A leaner version than the original orchestral recording.

365) Graceful Ghost Rag (William Bolcom) Lise De La Salle. Rec Berlin, 2020. From When Do We Dance? Naïve label (France).

A Bit of Brit

Romanza: Lento movement from Vaughan Williams' Fifth Symphony. "More than debatably his most purely beautiful . . . a symphony about hope" —David Allen/*New York Times*/October 16, 2022. I'd gravitate first to Sir Adrian Boult and Bernard Haitink's versions.

God Rest Ye Merry Gentlemen. From A New Orleans Christmas Carol on ELM label. 2002 Ellis Marsalis & Co.

Fun City (John Barry), 1969. From Midnight Cowboy Soundtrack.

Crazy Man Michael (Richard Thompson). Both live and studio versions (Fairport Convention/Liege and Leaf).

Feeling Good (Bricusse-Newley) Stanley Turrentine, Blue Mitchell, James Spaulding, Pepper Adams, Grant Green, McCoy Tyner, Bob Cranshaw, Mickey Roker, 1966. Arranged by Duke Pearson. From the album Rough 'N Tumble on Blue Note.

We Have All the Time in the World (John Barry/Hal David), 1997. From Shaken and Stirred/The David Arnold James Bond Project 1997 featuring Iggy Pop.

MP3 addendum to The Touch of Your Lips (Ray Noble), 1975. Also on The Tony Bennett/Bill Evans album Fantasy/Concord 2006 (alternate take).

The Pound is Sinking (Paul McCartney), 1982. From the album Tug of War.

Greensleeves. From Ben Weofter plays Ballads on Storyville label.

Polythene Pam (Unplugged). From The Beatles and Esher Demos

Into Miami (John Barry) From Goldfinger soundtrack 1964 EMI/Capitol. As the huge jetliner hits the runway, accompanied by a bold jazz waltz.

One Of These Things First—Nick Drake

Lagniappe

Tony Bennett's original "World on a String" from Bennett Sings a String of Arlen album is worth the strings attached. Bel canto. My ears, attitude and stereo have acclimated to "Isn't This a Lovely Day?" on Bennett/Berlin from 1987. Alec Wilder called it an "ingenuous little song," (Unsophisticated, artless, straightforward, candid). "Let the rain pitter patter but it really doesn't matter if the skies are gray; long as I can be with you it's a lovely day." Both on Columbia.

A strand of Streisand's: Absent Minded Me, the first track on the album People (Jule Syne and Bob Merrill). Arr: Peter Matz, 1964. I Had Myself A True Love (Arlen/Johnny Mercer). Arr: Sid Ramin. No noodling; a terrific tapeworm from The Third Album. The crescendo ending "When the Sun Comes Out" from Streisand's Second Album on Columbia is well-earned. Arr. By Peter Matz.

Three Bacharach-David songs to savor: "Who Is Gonna Love Me?" "Who Gets The Guy," and "Walk The Way You Talk." From Dionne Warwick—The Complete Scepter Singles.

Bill Evans' "Alice in Wonderland" and (I Love You) Porgy. From Sunday at the Village Vanguard and Waltz for Debby albums respectively, are best heard in the dark, with the soft crush of the ice, the joyous laughter of a young woman in "Porgy," enhancing the performance with the club ambiance.

Ditto Ray Charles' studio recording "At the Club" on Atlantic. . . . The clink of a shot glass during Oscar Peterson's "Ill Wind" from The Trio Live at the London House in Chicago on Verve, O. P.'s "A Train" from In Russia lp for its excitement and "Do You Know What It Means To Miss New Orleans" from the same recording; a delicious duet.

Ella Fitzgerald's "Bei Mir Bist Du Schoen" on Decca is brilliant; her introduction to Roy Eldridge on "You'd Be So Nice To Come Home To", in 1964, a pleasure day Lyricist/writer Gene Lees died, I found myself in an elevator with my boss and his haberdasher, singing them the lyrics to "Quiet Nights" as we descended from the third floor to the first. Phil was not impressed and fired me several years later for another sour note.

Lees wrote the English lyrics to Quiet Nights, Waltz for Debby, Desafinado, Song of the Jet, Someone to Light Up My Life and Double Rainbow. His essay "Um Abraco No Tom Antonio Carlos Jobim from his book Singers and The Song II is saudade on the page.

> The samba is basically a Negro-European thing. It has roots very similar to the jazz roots . . . But samba is the mainstream, the main road. Bossa Nova could be called a branch, one of the many branches that samba has . . Bossa Nova came with a very detached beat that cleaned the whole thing. And maybe because of that it became more universal
>
> —Tom Jobim, *Singers And The Song II*

Three highlights from Joao Gilberto in Tokyo/2002/Verve: Doralice, Isto Aqui o Que E? and Bolinha de Papel. Just Joao, in his best format, unaccompanied. Evolved.

> His performance is a ritual of simplicity. Mr. Gilberto simply walks onstage, sits down with his guitar and sings so gently that a hush falls over the room, and time itself seems to hold its breath.
>
> —Jon Pareles, *New York Times*, June 24, 2008,
> "A Seductive Urban Sound Hushes Carnegie Hall"

Gal Costa died in November 2022 at the age of seventy-seven. Jobim said she had good chops. Memorable tracks would include "Janelas Abertas" on Lumiar (Nice video of this), "Caminhos Cruzados" and "Se Todos Fossem

Iguais a Voce" from Antonio Carlos Jobim and Friends on Verve. Her great version of Candeias is also on CD: A Arte De Gal Costa.

Ao Amigo Tom (Marcos Valle-Paulo Sergio Valle-Osmar Milito) Claudette Soares, 1975. From A Musica de Marcos Valle E Paulo Sergio Valle on Universal/Mercury.

Terra De Ninguem (Marcos Valle-Paulo Sergio Valle) Marcos Valle and The Golden Boys. Smashing! 1968. From The Essential Marcos Valle compilation. Would splurge on the Japanese import of the original CD—Viola Enluarada Arr. Antonio Adolfo.

It's You Or No One (Jule Styne/Sammy Cahn) Sonny Stitt, Lou Levy, Leroy Vinnegar, Mel Lewis, 1959. From Saxophone Supremacy or Sonny Stitt/Four Classic Albums on Avid Jazz.

O Amor E Chama (Marcos Valle-Paulo Sergio Valle), 1968. From marcos valle/Viola Enluarada EMI/Odeon arr. Eumir Deodato.

Suave Asi (Tito Puente) Tito Puente, Bernie Glow, Ray Barretto, Carlos "Patato" Valdes, Jose Mangual, Santos Colon et al., June 25, 1959, New York RCA.

Chovendo Na Roseira (Tom Jobim) Tom Jobim, Edu Lobo, Luiz Claudio, Paulo Jobim, Luiz Alves, Paulo Braga, and Marcio Montarroyos, 1981. From Edu and Tom on Polygram do Brasil. Ltda.

E Preciso Dizer Adeus (All That's Left Is to Say Goodbye) (Jobim-deMoraes) Tom Jobim, Edu Lobo, Luiz Claudio, Luiz Alves, Paulo Braga, 1981. From Edu and Tom.

Spotlight on Dean Martin (Capitol) is a superb compilation. Definitive versions of "All I Do Is Dream of You," "The Things We Did Last Summer," "Wrap Your Troubles in Dreams," "Imagination," "Someday You'll Want Me to Want You," "Just In Time," "Until The Real Thing Comes Along," and "Hit The Road To Dreamland."

Ditto: bossa nova lounge/Ipanema on Dubas label. Marvelous Menescal/Boscoli, Luiz Eca, Marcos and Paulo Valle, Jobim, Ze Keti, Edu, Baden, and Milton.

A Piano Man's Fan: Ellis Marsalis' piano sounds warm, inviting and thoughtful, like the man. Growing up in New Orleans, I would see Ellis five rows behind me at the Prytania movie theater and annoy him with jazz talk, as fans are wont to do (before the projector rolled).

When Ellis' trio was performing at a by-gone Tyler's Beer Garden on Magazine Street, Wynton walked in, sat in the empty chair at my table, kept his head down, listening, sharing that he didn't care for that particular tune. I never forgot this mundaneness; Wynton was early in his ascendancy.

I got to know the man and his music a bit more after Hurricane Katrina. Every Friday night, at Snug Harbor jazz club on Frenchmen Street, Ellis would play Johnny Mandel's Emily, Cole Porter as sophisticated as Bill Evans, teeming with ideas in his improvisations. He told bedtime stories by Herbie Hancock, served up Fats Waller like a seafood-stuffed mirliton, offering several Waller standards in the performance. The joint wasn't jumpin' but full and appreciative. At the end of a work week in the flood-ravaged city, the Ellis Marsalis Quartet was balm for the soul.

When Ellis played his wonderful composition "Syndrome" at the outset, the audience was sold; one felt at home. Ellis' foursome played at a French Quarter Festival in the spring of 2010 in Jackson Square, plush with pink azaleas and surrounded by the oldest apartment buildings in the United States. The group played "Just You, Just Me" and I was satiated with French Quarter Fest, in that moment, for life.

Another special memory was Ellis inviting/driving me and a young drummer to Baton Rouge to hear Wynton and the Lincoln Center Jazz Orchestra. We played a little Sinatra with Sweets Edison on the drive up and Ellis engaged joyfully with the band before the concert. We went to see Wynton, ironing his shirt, accompanied by his bassist. I was a bit tongue tied; Wynton was gracious. The concert hall was full, the performance fine, the pianist professional. After intermission, Ellis disappears and is introduced to open the second half. Standing ovation. He intros with a soulful blues, gravitas resounding. I became a wallflower afterwards. Wynton asked if I was a critic. Just a fan, I offered, with a buss on the cheek. Speeding home, we get pulled over by a state trooper. "Officer," I speak up, "this man just got a standing ovation in Baton Rouge and his son received the key to the city," as he looked at the license. . . . On our way home, Ellis stopped for gas and donuts. I didn't take one and still regret that.

Years later, Jefferson Parish is commemorating the site on River Road where Marsalis Mansion once stood, hosting Ray Charles, Dinah Washington, and others that toured here during segregation. The Parish

President was there, along with Ellis' family, friends and fans.

Ellis once played David Raskin's "The Bad and the Beautiful," perfectly, on request. His live versions of "My Shining Hour" outshone Coltrane's Atlantic version from the early 60s. He has played the best "I Can't Get Started" I have heard, transforming a boring vehicle into a brooding noir piece, accented with light brushes. His "Invitation" (Bronislau Kaper) is always a kaleidoscopic seduction. I learned a lot more than music from Ellis Marsalis.

For the Record . . .

To Radio Center on South Claiborne Avenue, across from the Rex den, in New Orleans, where owner George Marcuse executed my first albums order. One Saturday morning in December, Fats Domino sauntered in, glittering in between the refrigerators. I recall Santana's first Columbia LP fronting the record bin. Later, Saturdays would have found me at Lenny's on Harrison Avenue, listening to Blood Sweat and Tears' "More and More." Lenny had thick, dark, slicked back hair, good air conditioning, and a good turntable in suburban 1960s Lakeview.

To Record Ron, who loved Joe Williams.

To Pat Berry's wonderful store—Leisure Landing—originally on St. Charles Ave., where Berry put David Grisman's first album—David Grisman Quintet—in my hand.

To The Dusty Groove in Chicago, where one could stroll afterwards, Sony Walkman in hand, to the benches of the Art Institute, listening to Oscar Peterson's Trio play "Ill Wind" from Live at the London House, in Chicago.

To the newly opened Virgin Megastore in Times Square, where Astor Piazolla blasted from speakers in the international section on the third floor. Listening to Ellington's "Harlem Air Shaft" while walking around the Village Vanguard at night.

To the Copadisco on the Avenida Atlantica, where the clerk spun Jorge Ben's "Que Maravilha."

To the bygone Modern Sound in Ipanema, a bossa nova mecca.
To Smiths on St. Charles, by the Pontchartrain Hotel, ruled by Alan Smason's mother, stocked with Capitol's songwriter series.
To Lippy Mawby at Magic Bus, Lefty at Euclid by the arch,
To Snooks and the gang at Louisiana Music Factory on Frenchmen Street.

Thanks also to Donna Kay Berger, Michael Lanaux, Bob and Laure Mineo, Corinne Morrison, sister of Randy Morrison, daughter of Chep Morrison, New Orleans Public Library Nora Navra Branch, Mid-City New Orleans Library, Steve Rueb, Stephen Caplan, Leon Weill, Paige and Joshua Pailet at A Gallery for Fine Photography, Nina Kooij, and Les White, my friend and sounding board.

You have to sluice through a lot of silt to get to the gold.
—Gary Giddins

A house is not a home.
—Bacharach-David

A computer is not a stereo.
—Editor